To:

Eleanor

From:

Jenn

Bali 2008

ISBN: 0-88396-946-7

Certain trademarks are used under license.

Manufactured in China.
First Printing: 2005

♻ This book is printed on recycled paper.

Blue Mountain Arts, Inc.
P.O. Box 4549, Boulder, Colorado 80306

A Little Bit of...

FRIENDSHIP

Blue Mountain Arts®

Boulder, Colorado

A Friend
Is One of Life's
Most Beautiful
Gifts

A friend is a person
 you can trust,
who won't turn away
 from you.
A friend will be there
when you need someone,
and will come to you
when they need help...

A friend will listen
even when they don't
understand or agree
with your feelings;
a friend will never try
to change you,
but appreciates you
for who you are.

A friend doesn't expect
too much
or give too little;
a friend is someone
you can share
dreams, hopes, and
feelings with. . .

A friend is a **per**son
you can think **of**
and suddenly **sm**ile;
a friend doesn'**t** have to
be told that
they are specia**l**,
because they kn**o**w
you feel that **way**.

A friend will
bend over backwards
to help you pick up
the pieces
when your world
falls apart.
A friend is one of life's
most beautiful gifts.

— Luann Auciello

Friends are angels
sent down to earth
to make good days
and to help us
find our way.

— Ashley Rice

A friend is
a one-in-a-million find,
the pot of gold at the end
of the rainbow,
a treasure that gives you
wealth untold.

— Vickie M. Worsham

Friendship
Is a Joy
That Never
Ends

Friendship begins with
meeting someone along the
path of life. Someone you
get to know, and gradually
get to know even better.
You discover what a joy it
is to spend your moments
with this person...

Friendship is sharing
thoughts and feelings
in a way that never felt
very comfortable before.
It is complete trust that
is sweetened with a lot
of understanding and
communication.

Friendship is a gift
that continually gives
happiness. It is strong
and supportive, and
few things in all the
world will ever compare
with the joy that comes
from its wonderful bond.

— Mia Evans

Some Friends
Are Forever

Sometimes in life,
you find a special friend:
someone who changes
    your life
by being a part of it.
Someone who makes
you believe there really is
    good in the world.
This is forever friendship…

When you're down,
and the world seems
dark and empty,
your forever friend
lifts you up in spirit
and makes that dark
and empty world
seem bright and full.

Your forever friend
gets you through
the hard times,
the sad times,
and the confused times.
If you turn and
walk away,
your forever friend
follows...

If you lose your way,
your forever friend
guides you
and cheers you on.
Your forever friend
holds your hand
and tells you that
everything is going
to be okay.

If you find such a friend,
you feel happy and
   complete,
because you need not
   worry.
You have a forever friend
   for life,
and forever has no end.

— Laurieann Kelly

You Are
a Perfect
Friend

You have known me
in good and
bad times
You have seen me
when I was happy
and when I was sad...

You have listened to me
when what I said
   was intelligent
and when I talked
   nonsense

You have been with me
when we had fun
and when we were
miserable...

You have watched me
laugh
and cry
You have understood me
when I knew what
    I was doing
and when I made mistakes

Thank you for
believing in me
for supporting me
and for always being ready
to share thoughts together
You are a perfect friend

— Susan Polis Schutz

We are all travellers in
the wilderness of this
world, and the best that
we find in our travels is
an honest friend.

— Robert Louis Stevenson

The world is empty if one thinks only of mountains, rivers, and cities; but to know someone who thinks and feels with us, and who, though distant is close to us in spirit, this makes the earth for us an inhabited garden.

— Johann Wolfgang von Goethe

There's No One
Else like You

There are rare people
   in this world
who are so caring —
whose natural instinct is
to put someone else's needs
   ahead of their own;
who are always there
   to listen
with a smile and
   a loving, open heart...

There are rare people
who never want or expect
praise for their good deeds
because that's just
    the way they are.

You are one of
those rare people...

How fortunate I am
that you are my friend!

— Andrea L. Hines

Friends
Make the World
a Better Place

Friends are the joys
that make us more
   like family
and the moments that
   show us
we still live in
   a caring world...

Friends are
the added strength we need
to face what life may bring;
they are always close
   at hand,
bringing hope to the soul.
They have arms full
   of caring;
they are there to soften
   every hurt.

Friends are candles lit
  by one another;
they are the glow of time
  and memory
to warm our hearts.

— Linda E. Knight

Friendship cheers like a sunbeam; charms like a good story; inspires like a brave leader; binds like a golden chain; guides like a heavenly vision.

— Newell D. Hillis

Of all the things
granted us...
none is greater
or better
than friendship.

— Pietro Aretino

You Are
Such a
Good Friend

You are the one person
Who shares my
   deepest thoughts
And loves me
   in spite of them...

You counsel me when
    my heart is broken,
And you stand by me
    when I'm mistreated.
You rally behind me in
    my good decisions
And are there to help me
Through the consequences
    of the bad ones.

Whom else can I call
At any hour of the day
   or night?
Who else accepts and
Understands all of me?
Not many people are
As blessed as I am
With someone like you
   in their life...

I don't know why
I was given
The wonderful gift of you
    as my friend,
But I'm grateful.
No matter what comes along
It brings me great comfort
To know that I can
    always count on you.

I hope you know
  in your heart that
I am that same sort of
  friend to you.
Our secrets are safe and
Our hearts are protected
Because of the love
  between us...
Two special friends.

— Pamela Malone-Melton

Friends
like You
Come Along
Once in a
Lifetime

Friends like you are so valuable and so rare. You provide me with things that can't compare with any other happiness in my life...

You understand my difficulties and always give me the benefit of the doubt. There are so many times when you're the only one who knows what I'm going through. You're what trust and communication are all about.

If you sense that
I'm hurting, you do
whatever you can to help
me. You walk beside me
when I could use a little
guidance and direction
in my life. You support
me in my attempts to do
what is right...

You multiply my smiles
and constantly add to
my favorite memories.
You make me feel like
I am somebody who
matters. Then you
quietly prove to me how
beautiful that feeling is.
I wish I had a way to
thank you for all this.

In you, I have come across a wonderful, once-in-a-lifetime friend. The gift of that friendship is the nicest thing anyone could ever give... and I will cherish it all the days of my life and all the years that I live.

— Emilia Larson

Thanks for Giving Me the Gift of True Friendship

❀

True friendship is that unexplained heart connection between two people who enrich each other's life. They may not know exactly why they became friends, but they do know that their presence in each other's life is a gift...

True friendship is one of the most valuable treasures anyone could have. It is nourishment to the heart and soul. It creates a feeling of unconditional acceptance between two people who allow each other to be themselves — just as they are.

This is our kind of friendship... the kind that exists between two people who understand each other and know how to communicate with each other.

Thanks for giving me the gift of true friendship.

— Donna Fargo

We wish to thank Susan Polis Schutz for
permission to reprint "You Are a Perfect
Friend." Copyright © 1984 by Stephen
Schutz and Susan Polis Schutz. And
PrimaDonna Entertainment Corp. for
"Thanks for Giving Me the Gift of True
Friendship" by Donna Fargo. Copyright ©
2003 by PrimaDonna Entertainment Corp.